BLESS

Love,
Lissa

I CAN ENTER YOUR LIFE

IF YOU LET ME

BY

ROBERT RAYMUND

www.mycatholic.life

Dedication

To my wife for providing the encouragement for me to publish these writings. To my son who provided a means of publishing this book and to all my family members. To a daughter in heaven who did her part in inspiring me. To a few friends who read these pages, edited them, and were inspired by these writings.

To our Lord Jesus Christ who gifted me with the ability to listen to the words of the Spirit.

May these writings glorify the name of Our Lord Jesus Christ.

•

By Robert Raymund

"Robert Raymund" is the pen name chosen by this author—Robert being the author's Confirmation name, and Raymund for the calling of Saint Raymund of Peñafort's blessings upon this work.

At an early age of twenty, Saint Raymund was teaching philosophy. He earned degrees in civil and canon law by his early thirties. Saint Raymund's abilities were of such high degree that kings, popes, and bishops all requested his service. Pope Gregory IX won his favor, and Saint Raymund of Peñafort made a lasting contribution to the Church by organizing a huge compendium of Church law, which served as a basic reference for canon lawyers until the twentieth century.

This author has prayed a daily novena to Saint Raymund for years, asking for special protection over life's events.

Saint Raymund, teach and assist us this day with wisdom needed to confront all the challenges we face in this life. Provide us with your intercession. Be with us as we pass from this world to the heavenly kingdom awaiting us.

Table of Contents

Introduction

While attending and presenting a religious couples' weekend, I took some time to write a letter to my spouse. While writing that letter, I suddenly wrote the words "*I can enter your life if you let me*" in the notebook I was using. I was surprised and deeply shaken as soon as I wrote them, because I knew they were not a part of my letter to my spouse, but were words that God was communicating directly to me. At the same time, I felt an overwhelming feeling of peacefulness as I had never experienced before.

When we returned home, I was able to continue writing reflections of a spiritual nature anytime I quieted myself, prayed, picked up a notebook, took pen in hand, and started to write. When I would write, it seemed that the words would flow out at about five times the speed I would usually write. I did not have to even think about what came out of my mind. The words just flowed out. At a later date, I clearly heard the words spoken to me: "*You will write a book, and it will be read by many.*"

The writings within this book are a result of these efforts for the next several years. I believe this is from God because when you encounter a deep sense of peacefulness, you just know it is bestowed from above and not of this world.

I struggled with this gift for many years and still do. This gift was stamped within me, and I always knew it was present. It never left. It was permanent. During that time period, several friends typed these reflections from my original notebook text, but we could not determine how to publish the contents. I asked God to help and to show the way when the correct time would arrive. Thirty-seven years passed before a path to publishing became apparent. I am thankful for this, as it fulfills the instruction I received.

My hope is that this book will be well received by many and that its inspirations will create many positive benefits. The best advice that I received over time was to *judge it by the fruits it creates*.

I know that this writing ability is a true gift from God that must be handled carefully and respectfully. Pride cannot enter and humility must prevail. The weakness to be aware of is putting yourself into it instead of listening to the depths of your heart. Someday, I pray that I am able to resume this writing being guided by the Holy Spirit. I leave this decision to the influence of the Spirit.

Land of the Lord

THE LAND OF THE LORD

Your difficulties will pass.
Your troubles will vanish.
Your confusion will diminish.
Your hope will grow.
Your heart will be filled with holiness,
    as you place your life into My hands.

Do not let fears prevent your surrender.
Do not let anxiousness distract you from Me.
Do not let selfishness mislead you.

I AM the goal you search for and desire.
I AM the force you crave and seek.
I AM the ending you wish for.

Let yourself go and surrender your life to Me.
Push aside what restricts and misguides you and join Me.
Let Me lift you into the zones of My lands.

My house awaits your entry.
My servants have prepared your room.
Your name has been listed with those from other times.
Your place with Me awaits you.

Let your expectations be lifted and trust in My Word,
    as you belong to My land.
Look forward to this event and live each day,
    knowing your place with Me awaits you.

BE WITH ME ALWAYS

Be with Me always and let My peace fill you.
Look to Me for your strength,
   as I will provide this for you.

What do you seek and search for?
Am I not enough as I AM and do I not provide for you?

Search for Me in all that you do
   and trust that I will be present.

Look always to Me for your strength,
   as I will be present to you.
You are My children,
   and I will care for you in all ways.

What concerns then should you have?
What fear should you possess?
Come to Me with all that you are.

Let go of your fears,
   as fear will not set you upon My path.
Let go of what you think you should be.
I accept you in all ways.

I AM your Lord and Master.
Let Me come into your life and set you free.
Let Me surround your life and give you life abundantly.

Let Me bring peace to your heart.
Treasure this time with Me.

COME INTO MY LAND

Come to Me for all that you desire.
Look for Me in all that is.
See Me in all that is present.
Expect My presence in all that is coming.

Do you fear My presence?
Do you run from Me?
Do you avoid involvement with My Spirit?

Place your avoidant behavior aside
   and come into My presence.
See My hand and how it welcomes and guides your path.
Trust its guidance and submit to its directions for you.

Do you await signs and symbols?
Does your blindness to these cause doubt?
Listen and hear Me.
Look and see My direction for you.
Trust and know that I am with you.

If this is true,
   then what question, doubt, or fear
   should remain with you?
If this is true,
   then what path do you follow?

DESIRE

What peace do you find from your adventures?
What adventures bring you contentment?
Does peace pass through your direction?

Does unrest find you at its mercy?
Lead your life to Me and seek its contentment.

My gifts are for you.
My life is with you.
Seek its favor.
Look for its behavior.
Have its blessing
    and discover its message that awaits you.

Choose your Master and become My follower.
Let your heart's burdens go.
Let My Spirit come to you
    and reach into your heart.
Become My son or daughter,
    and I will become known to your desire.
Listen to My whisper and hear My desire for you.
Let your adventure find its home with Me.

LET ME USE YOU

Give what you have to those who have nothing,
    and you will be blessed.

Let Me use you as My servant
    for those who need to be attended to.

Let Me give you what others need,
    so they may receive Me through you.

Let Me use you to help those
    who need to hear words of comfort.

Let Me use you to help those
  who need to be peaceful.

Let Me use you to help those
  who need to be lifted up,
    so they may know I am present and will bring joy.

Let Me become a part of you,
  and I will use you.

Help with My work,
  and I will be present to you.

THE MASTER

Your desire for peace and fulfillment
  can be satisfied through reaching
  into the Master's heart.
Satisfaction can be temporarily found,
  but lasting endurance
  finds its place with the Master.

The Master does not refuse you.
He welcomes you.
The Master awaits you.

Would a Master refuse a gift from a servant
  that is difficult for him to offer?

What reservations do you have?
What obstacles remain?

Put these aside and deliver yourself to Me,
  as I await your gift each day.

Prayer

PRAYER

Your time belongs to you.
Share these moments with Me
  each time in prayer.
See Me in your prayers
  and feel My presence.
Let us draw nearer to one another.
Let us become known to one another.

Let this time with Me
  become your means to understand
  and begin to hear Me speak to you.
Listen to Me, as I am beside you.
Hear My words that I have for you,
  and you will know I am present.

Your time in prayer
  will let you understand what I have given you
  and what you can do with these gifts.
Listen to My guidance
  and do not fear that I will mislead you.
Search for My direction within your prayers,
  and you will find your answers.

Let Me touch
  and become known to you.
Let Me guide you
  when you cannot find a way to Me.
Give yourself up to
  and depend upon Me.
Bring your burdens to Me.
Give up your independence.

Do not hide from Me,
  as I am next to you.

Let Me become known.
End your search
  and find your treasure.
Become rich in Spirit.
Its wealth will cover you.

Ask for this,
  and you will be given it.
Seek this,
  and you will find its treasure.
Find its treasure,
  and you will know its Master.

FREE ME

Bestow upon me Your wisdom.
Oh Lord, give me Your grace,
  as I await Your kingdom.

Let Your Face glow upon my eyes
  so that I might see You clearly.
Bring me life, Lord,
  so that I may serve You.

I do not know how to approach You.
Teach me, Lord,
  so that I may know You.
Free me, Oh Lord,
  so that I may be with You.

GOALS

Spend time in prayer,
   as this is the way for you to enter into My ways.

Seek My presence with you,
   as this is the way for you to be strengthened.

Gain strength from My presence,
   as this is the way for you to endure the events
   that take you away from My presence.

Do not complicate your goals,
   as you should focus upon only one:
   becoming more present to Me.

All other activities should follow this direction.

PRAYING

Talking to Me is the way I can help you understand
   what you face in your lifetime.
It should be a peaceful time that is spent with me.

We need to know one another on an intimate level.
Do this by talking to Me and listening, seeing,
   and being aware of work I perform around you.

This is My way of showing you
   that I want you to be happy and joy filled.
Your prayer should be open and peace filled.
Spend time with Me so you can know Me deeply.

I will give you many signs and blessings
   to help you become more confident with your prayers.

Do not be afraid of placing your burdens with Me,
   as they are small in My eyes.

Increasingly, I will help you ask for more.
Tell Me you love Me and live this love for Me.
This can be done with those around you.

Do not become selfish or impatient
   with your time with Me,
     as this will not lead to My peace.

SET ME FREE, OH LORD

Set me free, Oh Lord, set me free.

Soften my heart, Lord, soften my heart.
So I might know You, Lord, know You.

Let me know You love me, Lord, love me.
Let me know so I might hear You, Lord, hear You.

Comfort me, Lord, comfort me.
So I might be with You, Lord, be with You.

No matter what I do or say,
   You are always with me, Lord, with me.

No matter what, Lord,
   You are always at my side, Lord, at my side.

Give me peace, Lord, give me peace.

Open my mind, Lord, open my mind.

Be with me always, Lord, be with me.
So I might know You, Lord, know You.

Make me Your servant, Lord, make me.
So You will help me Lord, help me.

Be with me always, Lord, be with me.

WORSHIP

Take time to worship.
Let this time of praise be comforting.

Bring your soul to Me for My blessing.
Let this time deliver you unto Me,
 for I await your presence.

Set yourself free from distractions
 and place your soul with Me,
 for My grace will reward your effort.

Time with Me is sacred.
Time with Me will bring peace.
Time with Me will place your mind at a new cornerstone
 for you to hear what secrets await you.

Your time with Me will be rewarded with blessings
unknown to you,
 for you are My child,
 and I will care for you.

Trust

TRUST

May you be encouraged through your difficulties.
May you be lifted from your despair.
Believe and take comfort in Me.

I will take your burdens from you.
I will ease your pain.
I will bring you hope.
Let your troubles go.

Give these things to Me.
I will take them from you.
I will set you free.

Do not hesitate.
Do not delay.
I will set you free.

Do not wait.
Do not fear.
Let your mind be free.

I will give you the strength you need
    to endure your difficulties.
I will give you all that you need.
Trust in this promise.

ABOUT TIME

Use your time to know Me.
Hear Me and let Me give Myself to you.
I give you time to use.
I give time for you to enjoy.
Be peaceful with this gift.

Guide your gift of time
   with the direction I bring to you.
Listen to the words I speak to you through others.
Take these words of wisdom from Me
   and guide your precious time with this knowledge.

Do not try to understand all things,
   as you will grow tired from these efforts.
Be willing to trust the words of wisdom
   that are given to you.

Let go of your mistrust
   that does not lead you toward Me.
I will not injure you.
Trust Me as a child does her mother and father.

Let Me lead you.
Let Me help you.
Let Me bless you.
Let Me heal you of mistrust.
Let Me have your time.

If you do this,
   I will give you all that is blessed
   and unknown to you.

ALLOW ME

Your path leads to Me.
Your voice speaks My praise.
Your eyes look to Me.

I hear your pleas.
I listen to your questions.
I answer your needs.

Be at peace with My way.
Accept its course,
    as it leads others to Me.

You await a discovery of life's future.
Know that you will see My hand at your side.

Accept My will for your situation,
    as it fulfills My wish.

Be peaceful and bring your heart to Me.
Allow Me to work through you as needed.

CONTENTMENT

Look and see My plan.
Listen and hear My direction.

Watch and understand My control.
Enjoy and accept My presence.

What greater joy can you seek?
What greater satisfaction can be obtained?

What peace is more fruitful?
What end is more truthful?

Seek and find My truth.
Look for and discover My plan for you.
Enjoy My peace reserved for you.
Anything else will not bring you contentment.

DECISIONS

Do your decisions direct your course to Me?
Do they consider My words given to those before you?

Seek the examples given to you
    and set your course upon these directions.
Be patient with those who interrupt this path.
Be firm with those who follow false directions.

Seek My guidance,
    for it is given when asked for.
Trust that I will guide your path.

NO FEAR BELONGS

You have suffered much for My sake.
What comfort then can lift you?
What words then will soothe you?
What strength will protect you?

Have no concern about these questions,
    as all will be provided to you as needed.

Trust in My ways and methods,
  as My purpose will become known to you
  as My plan becomes fulfilled.

Do not concern your thoughts
  with fear for My purposes,
  as trust in My ways is all that is needed.

Your fear cannot help My purposes,
  as fear does not belong to My plan.

Take then a new look at My actions,
  as they will give you peace and contentment.

OBEDIENCE

Follow My ways set before you.
Let your path find its way in Me.

Place your course toward Me
  and do not let your path be misdirected.

Your course is set,
  and your sail will guide your path.
Your ship will bring you safely home;
  let this voyage belong to Me.

Your direction will lead you.
Your effort will sustain you.
Your course will please Me as your journey ends.
Your journey is fulfilled
  as you arrive at this journey's end.

Faith

FAITH

You are given many opportunities that call for faith.
These tests are given for your growth.
Always look for the good that is present
   within these experiences.

Do not let yourself be misled
   by the apparent displeasures
   that are visible to you.
Look beyond these apparent levels;
   look at the true meaning
   of My gift to you.
It is easy for a wise man to see this,
   but it is unclear to the ignorant.

Listen to Me when you are in doubt;
   I will help you to see the truth
   within these situations.

Do not be afraid to trust Me,
   for I will lead you to the destined place
   I have chosen for you.

Look for truth in others
   and trust those who are true to Me.
These people are gifted
   and will help you if you will allow them.

MY GIFT

Faith is My gift to you;
    let it fill you with hope and belief.
Do not doubt its power or result;
    let it fill you with grace.

You need not worry or fear;
    let your heart be filled with peace.
Let not a day pass without this peace.

With what, then, should your mind be concerned
    if you let this faith form you?
What then is it that can consume you?
What then will surround and threaten you?

Call upon this faith to be within you,
    and My peace will live within you.

BELIEVE

See My presence in your day.
Do you miss My grace?
Does it escape you?
Is it lost to your desire?
Has it left you?

I am present,
    but you cannot see.
I am with you,
    but you cannot hear.

Open your spirit to Me.
Let My grace enter you.
Let it surround you with its touch.

Trust and believe in My Word.
Free yourself of your doubt.
Let your mind rest without fear.
Believe in Me and enjoy the fruits of this peace.

DILEMMAS

You search for answers and find questions.
You find questions that have no answers.
What answers would please you?

Your faith is tested by these dilemmas.
Your search for truth is broadened
    through these experiences.
What do you do with these dilemmas?

Let your search for peace lead you
    to find comfort in Me.
I AM your answer.
Question Me;
    look to Me for your answers.

You need not know solutions
    for all of the events of your life,
    as this would bring you into My nature.

Recognize your human restrictions and have faith
    that I am a part of all that is beyond your knowledge.
Your faith is strengthened when you submit to Me.

Find what you search for in Me;
   I AM all that is.
Find the peace you search for in Me,
   as I will give you what is needed.
Find what you are in Me,
   as I AM what you searched for.

I AM what you are not able to understand.

I AM PRESENT

Each day brings news of My presence.
Look for these indications of My presence.
Become aware of My presence in your days.
I am there for you to discover.

These events will give you faith.
Look for them, see them, and enjoy them.
These happenings are My way of convincing you
   of My presence in all things.

When you have lost your faith,
   look for My presence each day
   and believe in what you discover.

When you have doubts,
   trust in My actions
   and have faith that I am with you.

When you are lost in your despair,
   have hope from My presence,
   as it will convince you of My goodness.

Do these, and your visions will become as Mine.

Your hope will focus on My goodness,
and your faith will stand any assault.

SPEAK TO ME

Speak to Me as you would a friend,
as I will listen to you as a True Friend.

Share your thoughts,
as they allow Me to nourish you.

Your selection of words needs not matter,
as the message of your heart is what is heard.

Speak truthfully,
so I may bless you with wisdom.

Speak out to Me,
so your confidence does not hinder your work.

Speak your heart,
for My treasures are bestowed upon you.

Hope

HOPE

Each day of the future
    brings new thought for you.
Consider each day's events
    as a new blessing for you.

The good days are welcome;
    the difficult days cause distress.
Learn to face each day
    with new hope and rediscovery.

Consider My guidance of your life's events
    when you are burdened.
I will not harm you.

Let your faith grow.
Let your hope give you peace.
Not a moment passes through you
    without My presence.

Take comfort in this
    as you face life's events.
Become aware of those who are not present to Me
    and help them reach into My presence.
Help them set their burdens free.

SEEING HOPE

What is seen can change.
What "is" will not have to remain.
See the hope beyond what is.

Ask and let it be.
Wait for Me to bring hope to be.
Let My hand let you see.

Count on My help for you to see.
For I am your light for you to be.
Let My light set you free.

You are what I care for.
You are for Me to set free.
Let My help bring you to Me.

I will touch your thoughts
  as you bring your heart to Me.
For I want to set you free.

A DAY TO REMEMBER

Each day presents new awareness.
Each day's treasure unfolds before you.

Look for the wealth that is present.
Admire each adventure as it is given to you.
Capture its benefits.
Enjoy its fruits.

Do not expect wrongdoing,
  as this will depress you.
See only My hand at work.
Let it encourage you.
Let it become your goal.
Let it belong to you.

I CARE ABOUT YOU

Your life on Earth is limited.
It was designed that way
  for you to realize
  and appreciate what is ahead of you.
Do not look back;
  only look forward
  to what awaits you.

You have made many mistakes with your actions.
If damage has occurred,
  repair the result of your mistake
  so you do not leave unnecessary injury behind you.

Look forward with anticipation of peace and joy.
This will lift you beyond your current status.
I will lead you to the joy I have for you,
  if you ask for this direction.

Do you think I will not help?
Do you think I cannot help?
Do you think you cannot ask for My help?
Ask and, on the correct occasions,
  it will be given to you.

Do not fear,
  as I will not hurt you.
Push aside your hesitations, fears, doubts,
  and any reason preventing you from seeking Me.

Seek Me with all of your desire,
  and you will be given all that you need
  for your joy and happiness
  during your lifetime on Earth.

This time can be a beginning of what is to come.
I want you to have this gift.

SATISFACTION

What hope exists but My hope?
What encouragement exists
   but My encouragement?
What love is stronger than Mine?

Not even a breath of air is meaningful
   without My guidance.
Not even a minute of your day is worthwhile
   without My direction.

Take to My way and see your path.
Seek My methods and understand your direction.
Accept My words and become aware of My plan.

Not a second passes
   without your view present to Me.
I am always within you.
Seek My presence
   and know that I am with you.
Become aware of My nature
   and know that I care for you.
Let My nature encompass your time
   to bring you satisfaction
   and contentment with each passing day.

Love

LOVE

What matters most
  is My love for you.
It is like the rain
  as its cleanses all
  it falls upon.
It is like the sun
  as it gives refreshment
  to all living.
It is like the air
  as it gives life to all
  that requires its nourishment.

If this is love's character,
  then receive its benefits.
Accept love's blessings
  and share its fruits
  with those who cross your path.

LOVE'S FRUITS

Love brings hope to those who are vacant.

Love is kind.
Love is gentle.
Love is freedom from despair.
Love helps to see the truth amongst confusion.

Give all and feel its return.
Take love's fruits without guilt.
Keep love's benefits without regrets.

Encourage each other's attempts.
Do not become discouraged from your failings.
Look for new life as it is given.
Let love's fruits tame your burdens.

A PROMISE

Just as the light of the sun warms the earth,
    I will give warmth to your heart.

I will comfort you in times of pain.
I will give you wisdom in times of confusion.
I will provide you hope in times of despair.
I will give you relief in times of pain.
I will soften your anger in times of injustice.
I will provide protection in times of persecution.

No anxiousness deserves your attention then,
    as I watch over you.
Do not let any fear grow within you,
    as My promises will not fail you.

MY LOVE

Reach out to those who need your help.
Do not think more of yourself
    than you do of others.

Become aware of who needs
    your care, understanding, and wisdom.

These gifts will be given to you
   as others need them.

Do not plan how you love one another,
   as I have given you this instruction in the Word.
Understand My Word
   and bring peace to others.

Look for the needs that you can fulfill
   with the talents and gifts I have given to you.
Use yourself in this way
   to glorify Me.

Care for those who need you;
   give them My peace as best you can.
I will help you do this
   for those whom I bring into your path.

MY TREASURE

Open your heart.
Let your troubles go.
For no trouble will devour you,
   as you walk with Me.

And what tragedies can devour you,
   as you look to Me?

No difficulties are too overbearing,
   and no injustice is irreversible.

I will save you from your helplessness,
   and I will change your fortune.

Follow My path and
  let My presence comfort you.

For you are My treasure,
  and no harm shall burden you.

WITHIN ME

Become centered in Me.
Cast out what distracts you.
Let My love encompass you.

Do not fear My presence,
  as I am gentle and will be kind to you.

Lift up your heart to Me,
  as this is the way for you to know Me.

Let My grace penetrate your heart
  and fill you with its healing touch.

Do not hesitate or hold back your submission,
  as I want you to belong to Me.

Let yourself be free and join your spirit to My grace.

Blessings

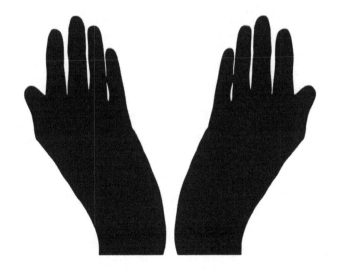

BLESSINGS

Blessings are given.
Blessings are received.

Blessings await those who are in need.
Blessings are received by those who need.

Blessings are from the Lord.
Blessings are for those of the Lord.

Blessings touch hearts of stone.
Blessings soften those in pain.

Blessings lighten burdens from unknowns.
Blessings give freedom from dark times.

Blessings lift hearts full of pain.
Blessings give life to those who suffer.

Blessings bring joy to those who are sad.
Blessings heal those hearts from pain.

ACCEPT ME, AND ALL THAT I AM IS YOURS TODAY

Reach out for Me.
Look for Me.
Let Me enter you.

Open your heart up to Me.
Let Me bring you peace.
Bring your fears to Me.

Open up your mind to Me.
Place your concerns upon Me.
Let your doubts go.
Let Me give you peace.
Let your fears go.

Become a part of Me.
Place yourself with Me.
Turn yourself over to Me.
Let Me live within you.
Let Me become a part of you.
Know and accept Me,
    and all that I AM is yours today.

I bring light and peace
    to those who seek these gifts.
I give joy to those who desire it.
Ask for these blessings,
    and they will be given.
Seek My life,
    and it will be shared with you.
Understand My words
    and enjoy their message.

Turn to Me with your heart,
    and you will know me.
Work for and become a part of Me.
All that I AM and all that I do
    will become known to you
    when you join Me.

DISCOVERY

No fear should stop you.
No hesitation deter you.
No doubt should prevent you
    from your time with Me.

No other effort is more important.
No other time spent is more fulfilling.
No other benefit is more rewarding.
Your time with Me is fulfilling,
    as you understand more of Me.

What gifts can be discovered?
What knowledge can become known?
For you are a vessel for Me to teach,
    and My Words will touch you with its grace.

INSPIRED

Be inspired
    by the gifts given to you.
Let these gifts
    touch others' lives.

I give you blessings
    to bestow on others.
This is My reason
    for the treasures that surround you.

As more and more of the poor of heart enter your life,
    be generous to them
    with the gifts I have bestowed upon you.

Let My grace flow out from your words and actions,
   so these poor at heart may be led unto Me.
What is given to them is My desire.

Let this path of My work
   suffer no interruption or loss.
With this sight you will serve My Word,
   and My kingdom is your resting place.

MY GIFT OF TIME

The time that I give to you is My gift.

When you are not of My Spirit,
   I am not with you.
These times are not Spirit filled for you.

Look to Me
   for the grace you need in your lifetime on Earth;
   this small cycle in your life
   is to be a grace-filled time.

Do not be afraid
   to extend yourself to Me.
This is My will.

When you consider the life you have
   and all of the aspects of this life that have been
planned for you,
   you should have joy.

Joy is what I have for you in the many forms
   that come to you in situations that this life gives you.

Enjoy these and fight against the negative emotions
   that deter you from this.

MY HAND

See My hand in all things.
It is always within the events surrounding you.
Look for My hand of guidance
   that determines and directs
   the events of your daily life.

Look and see My hand in all things,
   as it is present even in the most unobvious ways.
My presence within these matters can be discovered,
   if you listen, look, see,
   and feel the grace of My presence.

Do not be afraid to experience this grace,
   as it is unlike all that you now have.

Be willing and trust,
   as I will not hurt you or cause you
   despair, grief, anger, disappointment, or fear.

I am gentle with those
   who look for My direction, help, and grace.

Be one of My disciples and friends;
   I want you to belong to Me.
Give of yourself,
   and I will bless you.

QUIET TIMES

I speak to you in quiet times
  to let My Word be known.

These times are sacred times
  so you may know more about Me.

These times are needed for Me
  to inform you about what is wanted.

Let these times be filled with grace,
  as they are for your wisdom.

Spend time with Me
  so you will know My Word,
  and I will bless these efforts.

No concern is needed,
  and no fear should be present,
  as I AM your Savior who brings peace.

YOUR DAYS

The days of your life
  are given to you to enjoy
  and use for strengthening your soul and others.
This purpose is given
  so you may prepare for what is to come.

Your actions should be directed
  upon the work I have for you.
Search for this meaning and direction.

It is evident,
    if you are aware of My guidance.

Many signs are given to you
    so that your mistakes are diminished.
Become aware of how to read these signs,
    as they are given for a purpose.

The days I give contain many opportunities
    to help with My work.
You look for the most obvious
    and do not find me.
This is because you cannot hear Me.
Listen closely and patiently,
    as I am with you.

I am always with you,
    but you are not always with Me.
Direct your efforts
    so you are with Me more often.
This will bring you
    wisdom, knowledge, joy, and peace.

Listen to My whispers,
    and you will know what I want from you.
Come to Me
    and bring others with you.

Enjoy the blessings that await you.

Guidance

GUIDANCE

When you look to Me
   for direction and guidance,
   I will answer.
Do not anticipate the answers I will bless you with.

Listen to the signs and influences
   that are unexpected.
Pray often;
   this will help you
   to determine what is truth.

Do not overreact,
   as I do not place pressure
   on those who ask for My guidance
   and seek out direction from Me.

I will guide your life if you let Me.

ABOUT MONEY

Use your earnings to bring joy
   to those whom you support.

Do not worry about how much you have.
I will provide!

Be helpful to others,
   but do not place yourself
   into a position that will not help My work.
The poor will always be.

I do not measure holiness with wealth.
Use what I give to you wisely;
    I love and trust you.

Some are given much;
    some are given less;
    some are given nothing.
I make these decisions.

Some need much;
    others do not.
Some want much;
    others do not.
Some deserve much;
    others do not.
I give to all what is best for them.

Use what I give to you
    as generously as you judge.
Do not be driven
    by the world's desires.
Know and trust that what I give to you
    is for you to help bless those to whom you are closest
and those whom I bring to you for help.

Feed the hungry;
    give help to those who are poor.
These people await your help.

I give wealth to those
    who can serve others this way.
Some take wealth
    and do not serve Me.
This type of wealth will fail.
I will bless you when you help others.

COME TO ME

Bring life to those who have lost theirs.
Have trust as I guide you.
Do not fear or doubt as I guide you.
Look for My direction,
    and you will find it.
Seek My guidance,
    and it will be given.

I will help you
    as My work awaits your attention.
Fear will delay your actions;
    doubt will mislead you.
These are not from Me.

Be a child of Mine,
    and you will know Me.
You will be given all that is
    as you bring yourself to Me.
This awaits your decision each day.
Bring yourself to Me,
    and you will taste the fruits of My grace.

DIRECTION

When you consider the ways of the world,
    what it teaches you and how you are tempted,
    be aware that My teachings and wishes are different.

I have given you a way
    and will give you the grace
    to follow this way, if you ask.
I will not force you.

Be ready to consider the words
    I give to you through others.

You will see a pattern and,
    with your wisdom,
    will follow My way.
This will lead you to Me.

I will guide you
    with My words and direction.
I give this to you
    as a gift from Me.

I will show you what path to follow
    since you cannot always clearly determine
    what the path is that I wish you to follow.
I will do this for you
    when you ask for My guidance.

There are many directions
    that you can choose to follow.
I will provide you with the gifts
    that you will need
    to fulfill the plan that I have for you.

Be My child;
    help Me give peace and joy
    to those who want the gifts that I am eager to share.
When you do this for Me,
    you will experience the peace and fulfillment
    that is unlike the poems and writings
    of human dreams.
My peace will allow you to understand what awaits you.

DOUBTS

Trust My Words that lead you;
    abandon your false directions.
Place your trust upon My path
    and never doubt My love.
I will not mislead or harm you.

Do not then fear
    what is planned for you,
    as its course will guide you.
Do not be distracted
    by what appears to be painful.
But rejoice when life's burdens
    lead you to Me.

Any suffering, then, can bless you
    and help you live within Me.

GOODNESS

Focus upon the goodness
  you see each day.
Year after year these events
  are given for you to enjoy.
This is to convince you
  of My presence.
Even your difficulties
  contain goodness.

Look for these signs
  before you condemn the events you face each day.
Enjoy the fruits of these signs
  and believe in My goodness,
    as it is truth.

Each hour of the day
  offers a sign from Me.
Each day of your life,
  I am present.
Enjoy these events
  and trust that I am with you always.
Be strengthened
  by what you witness.

Believe in what you see.
Let your faith and hope
  be increased from My presence
  each day of your life.
Your concerns will diminish
  as your trust in Me grows.
Your faith will multiply
  as you accept My presence.

I AM ALWAYS WITH YOU

Your doubts
   will blind you.
Your fears
   will hinder you.
Your hesitations
   will mislead you.

Give these difficulties
   back to their Creator.

Desire for My nature
   will bring you upon it.

Your search
   will let you find Me.

Patience with your nature
   will allow you to understand Mine.

You will know My presence
   when you are open to My nature.

Ask for Me,
   and I will find you.

Reach out for Me,
   and I will be there with you.

Not a fragment of time
   will pass you without Me.
Not one event will begin
   and end without Me with you.

LET ME HELP YOU

When you consider the many trials
   that each of you encounter,
   how you solve them,
   and the results that you accomplish,
   the best you can hope for
   is a little success.

When facing life's trials,
   look to Me for help and direction.

Turn these decisions over to Me
   and let Me help you.
Look to Me for answers
   that you cannot arrive at.
I will give you the truth.

I am patient with your contemplations and attempts
   to be independent of My direction.
I know that you find it necessary to try on your own
  without My help.

I wait for you to ask Me for the answers
   that you cannot find.
Learn to ask for My help sooner
   than to what you are accustomed;
   do not look at this as failure or weakness.

Giving

GIVING

Bring peace to those who need comfort.
Give joy to those who are sad and burdened.
Give awareness to those who cannot see.
Bring hope to those who cannot understand.
Teach those who will listen.
Heal those who suffer.

Open the eyes of those who have closed them.
Open the hearts of those who have been hardened.
Give life to those who have despair.
Help those who want to be changed.
Encourage those who search for more.
Lead those who are lost.

I change those who desire more.
I shelter those who need comfort.
I enlighten those who ask for help.
I give peace to those who suffer.
I refresh those who need rest.
I bless those who help others.

Give to those who need your help.
Do not fear the difficulty you may have with this,
    as I will give you the courage
    and necessary gifts that you may require.

What you have can be given to others,
    and what you are will grow as I bless your efforts
    and give what is needed for those who are in need.

Do not be afraid of My work,
    as I will help you and strengthen you as needed.

Do not search for those in need,
   as I will bring them to you.

EACH DAY

Look for My presence in your day.
I am with you,
   but you do not recognize My presence.
Be convinced that I am with you.

Increase your faith in My goodness,
   and trust that I will help and guide you.
Your doubts will not increase your faith.
Your independence will not give you strength.

Set aside these obstacles
   that direct you away from your faith.
Give up your dependence
   upon what leads you away from Me.

Give yourself to those
   whom you meet each day.
Bring peace that comforts their concerns.
Offer wisdom to those in need.
Direct those who are misled.
Strengthen the poor in spirit
   so they may know Me.

Search for and desire these fruits
   so you may prosper and influence
   those whom your path crosses each day.

Let Me fill you with My gifts
  and let these benefits be given to others.
Influence those who need to understand
  more about My nature.
Let Me work through you
  and use you for this purpose.

HELP MY PEOPLE

Reach out to those
  who need to be helped.
Help those who need your assistance,
  as you have gifts to share
  with those who have less.
Be willing and trust that I will help you with this work.

Many needs exist for you to help with.
Choose those areas
  that your talents seem to be directed toward.
Let Me work through you and with you
  as you share your gifts
  with those who need help.
Be generous with what you share with others.
Many times,
  I bring those who need to be helped
  to those who can give help.

Help those who are not as knowledgeable
  or who have need of wisdom.
Listen to their words
  and give them direction.

Do not fear that you will not be able to provide this,
   as I will help you to give what is needed.

Step toward those who await this help,
   and all that you need will be provided.
Do not fear that you may not have what is needed
   to provide this service
   to those who are in need.
I give to each what is needed
   to fulfill My plan.

I bless those who trust in Me.

Peace is given to those who help
   and those who receive help.
Do not search out those
   who need to be given inspiration.
They will become present to you
   when their needs are to be fulfilled.
Be willing to help when these needs
   are presented to you.

OPPORTUNITIES

The days of your life on Earth
   are filled with joy, disappointment, hope,
   and the needs of others.

Use your time to show My grace
   to those with whom you spend your days.

Reach out to those
   who are in need of comfort.

Feed those
who need to be instructed.

Give wisdom to those
who need to grow in their awareness of Me.

Help those
who need your assistance.

I will reward these efforts.

Many opportunities for this work
are presented to you.

Do not be afraid of involvement,
as I will be with you
through any difficulties that occur.

Trust in My hand of guidance,
as it will be over you.

I am with your efforts
when you help My people grow.

My joy will enter you,
and I will bless your efforts.

Dedicate the days of your life
to working for My people.

I want to use you
to help those who need
encouragement, knowledge, wisdom, hope, and trust.

Let Me use you for this.

SELF GIVING

Be helpful to each other,
    as this is the way you can be blessed.
Use the time you have with each other
    for My work.
Be open to the grace I have to give you
    through each other.
Recognize My blessings when they are given
    and enjoy the fruits of each occurrence.

When you listen
    to My messages, instructions, guidance, and desires,
    you are blessed by My grace.
This is what I want from you.

Do not fear the results of My grace,
    as it is beyond your understanding.

Trust in My actions,
    as they are for your peace, enjoyment, and direction.

I will bless you
    with many signs that will increase your faith,
    if you yield to My wish for you to be blessed.

You need only to submit your life to Me
    without restriction or qualification.

Do this each day,
    as it is your sacrifice for Me.

This gift of your self-giving
    will be rewarded in many ways.

STRENGTHENED AGAIN

Be strong in your heart
  and gentle to the weak.
Give praise to Me
  without hesitation and doubt.
Speak My Words
  to those who need their comfort.
Be silent to those
  who choose not to hear.
Be patient with those who suffer,
  as they need to be understood.
Be kind to those who are anxious,
  as they are distracted from Me.

A heart filled with My grace
  will fill others who need to be blessed.
Submit to this purpose,
  and your soul will be strengthened again.

SUBMISSION

Patience with those who need to be heard
  brings joy to My plan.
Practice this with those
  whom I bring to you.
Their hearts are heavy
  and their burdens painful.

Help them to see Me more clearly.
Help them open their hearts,
  and I will bless them with peace.

Learn to recognize these needs in others
   and listen to their stories as I would.

My servant needs no other favor than Mine.
Be open to these favors,
   as you will rejoice many times from its blessings.
What is more important than My desire for you.

Submit to this,
   and I may use you for My purpose.
Submit to My purpose,
   and your troubles will be small.
Submit to My purpose,
   and peace will come from My blessings.
Submit to My purpose,
   and My heart belongs to yours.

Change

CHANGE

Renew yourself,
   as this change will prepare you
   for what awaits you.
Reach for this change,
   as delays will not bring you
   closer to Me.
Do not fear changes,
   as you will not be harmed.

Trust in Me;
   I will care for you
   during your period of change.

Look forward to My spirit
   lifting you, enlightening you,
   and coming upon you in many ways.

Surrender yourself.
No greater gift can be given to the Father.
Many blessings will be given
   to those who surrender
   their minds and hearts to Me.
A peace will be given to you;
   a joy unknown will cover you.
Surrender yourself,
   as this action
   will bring you into My kingdom.
You will know My word
   and see My presence around you.
You will find many reasons
   to delay your surrender.

What wisdom is found in your delay?
What gain can be found without Me?
What comfort exists without My Spirit leading you.
What goals have you reached without Me?
Look at what you are without Me
   and then realize what you are
   with My Spirit within you.
Let Me become a part of what you are,
   and you will know Me.
Surrender yourself,
   and I will be with you each day.

BECOME ANEW

Look for a difference.
Search for a change.
Reach out to a discovery.
Enjoy the event.
Find the fruits.
Share its result.
Become its end.

What matters in the end
   is not how you have begun
   but how you have changed
   from the discoveries given to you.

What matters in the end
   is what you have become
   from the fruits given to you.

What matters in the end
  is what you have become
  from My blessings.

What matters in the end
  is the understanding of Me.

COME CLOSER

Become a part of Me
  through your actions.
Each day presents a new opportunity
  for you to live your day as I did.
Take each day that you have
  and live it with your actions
  focused toward My words
  that I gave to those who have lived before.

Become like the examples
  that others before you have given.
Listen to those around you
  who are focusing their actions on Me.

Become a part of the truth
  that I AM.
Each day will bring you closer to Me
  if you live your life in this way.
Become a child of truth.

Become a child
  who has completed the search.
Look for Me,
  and you will find Me.

Search, and you will discover.
Ask, and I will be with you.
You will see My ways and know Me.

Your doubts will blind you,
  and your mistrust will lead you
  in other directions.
Do not let these obstacles mislead you.
Look for Me.
Search, and you shall find.
Ask, and you shall know.

LIFTED

What light do you see
  when you search for answers unknown to you?
Do your answers fall short
  of your desires for awareness?
Are you confused
  by your deliberations and uneasiness?

Recognize first your inability
  to solve life's questions.
Understand that only a little
  is expected of you.

If you carry a heavy burden,
  then release it.
Be lifted,
  as you recognize My light.
Enjoy its warmth and favor.
Be encouraged by its impression.

Let My light fill you
  with what is unknown to you.

Allow this.
Ask for this.
Expect this.

LOOK TO ME OFTEN

Look to Me for your joy and peace;
  these fruits will result
  if you live My Word.
Many questions arise,
  and many answers are unknown to you.
These answers can become a part of your understanding
  if you listen to the wisdom I give you.
This wisdom will help you to understand
  the direction that has been outlined for you.
Seek this direction,
  and it will be given to you.

Do not be fearful of change,
  as this is for your growth and development.
Look upon change
  as a gift from Me
  that brings your vision closer to mine.
Look upon understanding
  as a gift from Me.

Share your inspirations and wisdom with others
  so they may grow
  and become more understanding of Me.

Look to Me for strength,
   as I give you this blessing
   as you require it.
Ask for My grace to strengthen you.
Your strength will be used
   to lead others to Me.
Look to Me for answers to your questions.
I will answer
   if you come to Me with your questions.

The time you spend for Me is your offering.
You should look for ways
   that bring My people closer to Me.
You need not create new ways;
   many situations are already present
   for you to assist with.

Look for what already exists
   and contribute to these needs.
These needs will be apparent to you
   if you are aware they exist.
Look for ways to help others
   become more aware of Me.
Many opportunities will be presented
   to those who wish to contribute to this work.

Look to Me for your needed strength and direction.
I will bless you with these gifts
   when the need arises.
Look to Me for understanding of the complications that
you face each day,
   since you cannot always determine the true direction I
would have you follow for each trial that you encounter.

Look for this grace,
   and it will be given.
Take this truth
   and share it with those who are
   confused, misled, unaware, and poor in spirit.

Many times I speak to you in My word
   and show you signs, direction, and inspiration.
These words and guidance are for you
   to learn more about Me
   and direct your time on Earth.
Be serious with the guidance I provide;
   pray for this help.

Ask Me to help and guide you.
I want to help you.
I want you to depend on this help.
Many times I give you help when you do not ask for it.
Many times you reject the help I give to you.

Look to Me for all things,
   as I will provide all that you need.
Do not judge My blessings from what appears to you
   as discouragement or punishment.
Many times these apparent misfortunes
   are the most fruitful blessings that I give you.
Ask and look to Me for these blessings.

TROUBLES

Place your troubles upon Me.
I will take them from you.
Let go of your disturbances.
Give these things to Me.

When you search for answers
   and cannot determine what direction to lead yourself,
   place yourself with Me,
   and I will give you direction.
Do not hesitate or delay asking for My help,
   as it is for you.

Your doubts and reservations are necessary;
   but do not prolong these times,
   as you will be given My help as needed.
Ask for this help,
   and it will be granted.
Submit your doubts and fears to Me,
   and I will change you.

What benefits do you gain from your concerns?
Place these issues with Me,
   and I will give you peace.

Does a father reject a son who needs his help?
Does a mother ignore her baby when the baby is ill?
No. A father nurtures his son
   and gives him guidance
   so that he may not suffer.
A mother tends to her baby
   until the baby is well.
I will do the same for you.

TURN TO ME

You search for the unknown
 but do not find it.
Look for Me
 and find what you seek.

What joy do you find
 in what you do?
What happiness do you find
 in what you have?
What peace results
 from these events and wishes.

Turn your desire to Me
 and find your peace.
Turn your hope to Me
 and find your future.
Turn to Me with your heart
 and see My wish for you.
Turn yourself to Me
 and find the joy that awaits you.

Set your fear aside
 and replace it with hope.
Clear your mind
 of what keeps you from coming to Me.
Place your burden into My hands,
 and I will take it from you.

Bring your doubts to Me,
 as they will blind you.
A blind man cannot see
 with his lack of faculty.

When this obstacle is removed,
   he may see.
When your blindness is removed,
   you may see.
What blinders do you have?

When you search for Me,
   what do you find?
Does your blindness cause false vision?
When you see My hand at work,
   what vision of Me do you have?

I AM what you search for.

Wisdom

WISDOM

Life's events bring joy and confusion.
What is behind these happenings?
How do they develop and end?
What is contained within these two limits?
Understanding is not easy.

What wisdom is contained within
    and from the events that come upon you?
Look for this wisdom.
See its vision.
Use its direction.
Take comfort in its ending.

A PETITION

Petition My help, as it is for you.
Do not fear what awaits you,
    as I will let no harm find you.

Bring your petition to My throne,
    and I will grant your wishes.
I am generous with you,
    as I care about how your happiness pleases you.

What matters is not what others say is good for you
    but what desires you have for Me.
Let your desire for Me lead you
    from a status of reservation
    to that of an open yearning for My presence.

EXPECTATIONS

Your expectations can misguide your course.
Your behavior will follow a course.
Examine the path you follow.
Does it lead you to My house?
Does it bring you into My shelter?

Does the path you follow lead to Me?
Set your path toward My house,
    as I await your arrival.

Set aside that which will not help you.
Be encouraged with My desire for you.

Examine your course and direct it toward Me.
I will help you follow My path.

Trust in My help,
    as I will not misguide you.
Believe in My promptings,
    as this is for you.
Recognize My course for you and follow.

What fear warrants your attention?
What delay helps you?
I await your action.
Do this and have My guidance.

LEADING

Be patient with those who need to be heard.
Listen to those who need to speak.
Offer advice to those who lack wisdom.
Understand those who are confused.

Pray with those who need help.
Bring peace to those who suffer.
Give joy to those who seek comfort.
Give strength to those who are weak.

Prepare those who need to be lifted.
Correct those who are lost.
Pray for those who will not listen.

I AM the strength of those who seek more.
I AM the peace to those who want more.

MESSAGES

What messages do you receive,
    and how do you react to these demands?
A politician communicates his plan,
    searching for your loyalty.
A friend shares with you in search of your approval
    and advice.

My message to you is different than these.
It leads you, gives you comfort, and asks for change.
Is this not more important than the others you hear?
Is it not of a higher order?
Does it not ask and give more?

Many times this message is mixed
   with that of the social order.
This is good when achieved with wisdom from me.
Be aware of those who mix My word with the social
word for their benefit.
Be aware of those who manipulate these differences for
selfish gain.

A man who is pure in spirit
   has wisdom from Me
   and speaks My purpose.
Listen to his knowledge and guidance above others.
Learn to hear My words from those who seek no selfish
gain for their own benefit.

PRESENCE

See My hand present within your lifetime.
Let My influence be known
   as you become aware of this presence.
Let My presence lift you unto a new level
   of wisdom and peacefulness.
Rid yourself of the distractions that prevent you
   from being fully aware of My presence.

What greater joy can be gained than this?
What greater peace can be experienced than this?
Let these fruits become a part of you.
Let the awareness become present and known to you.

PROPHECY

Prophecy encourages with words of My choosing.
A prophet speaks My words;
   let them be heard.
His message communicates My nature;
   let this be known.

A word that encourages you
   will give honor to Me.
A direction understood
   will give Me glory.

The words of a prophet when heard
   bring you closer to My visions.

This pleases Me.

My words can be known to you
   as you understand what
  visions, guidance, and hope are given.

A prophet places himself in My trust,
   as this submission allows My nature to be known.
Let these experiences be given
   to those who listen
   and seek My words.
Let these words be given and known as mine.

WORK DAYS

Your work is for Me.
Keep this in mind as you labor each day.
Give a fair effort and expect fair treatment,
    as this is My expectation for those whom you labor.

Your work should not interrupt your time
    given to those closest to you and to Me.
Be generous with your work,
    but do not let it interfere with My work.

Suffering

SUFFERING

Many times I allow you to suffer much pain.
Look at these experiences as a blessing.

Your suffering will vanish
    as you surrender your pain to Me.
These experiences are growth for you,
    so I may lead you into the next phase of My plan.

Do not look back at your suffering.
A wise man understands.
He knows My goodness and understands
    that all he endures strengthens him in My service.

Choose which direction you follow,
    but understand that My ways
    are not always easily understood by all.
Choose My way,
    and you will be blessed.
Fear has no favor for you to bear
    when you follow My ways.

Your pain gives praise to Me
    when you realize that you suffer for My purpose.
Feel strength grow within you
    as you choose My way.
Let this peace enter you, fill you, lift you,
    and overflow onto those who cross your path.

ANXIETY

Each encounter with pain leads you to new discoveries.
Look at these experiences as necessary for your growth.

No pain will be overbearing.
No time of suffering will be excessive.
These experiences are a part of your human condition.

Welcome this anxiety,
    as it will lead you into a new wealth of awareness.
Do not give the pain attention.
Instead,
    welcome your new knowledge and understanding,
    as this is My hope for you.

Look always beyond your current pain
    unto the new growth prepared for you.
Look always unto the growth as another step
    toward that which awaits your attention.
Seek the change that has been prepared for you.
Delight in its fruits,
    as these benefits are for your happiness.
Enjoy this gift,
    as it has been reserved for your pleasure.

FOR THE SICK

Nourish those who are sick,
    as they cannot care for themselves.
What favors that you give them are pleasing to Me.
Let not your hesitations, fears, or resistance
    block your path.

Give to those who are ill,
  as this is My desire.
Let not your temptation be to look away,
  as they need your attention.
Give yourself to them,
  as this will please Me.

Give them peace and hope.
Listen to their fears and be patient with them.
Let yourself belong to them,
  as they need your attachment and presence.

TORMENT

Come to Me with your burdens.
Place them at My feet.
Give them to Me and let Me change you.

You suffer much.
Let Me help you.

When your mind is confused with turmoil,
  let Me release you from this.
I will lift you from your despair.
Let Me set you free.

Trust Me with this promise, as My desire for your peace
is greater than any torment you suffer.

TRUTH

I allow your suffering
  so you might understand
  more of the love I have for you.
I allow your pain
  so you might know more about Me.
I allow your sadness
  so I might comfort you.
I allow your confusion
  so I might give you hope.
I allow your frustrations
  so I might teach you patience.

YOUR PAIN WILL SET YOU FREE

Suffering brings life's reward.
Let suffering open your way to Me.
Let it wash your soul.
Let it free your spirit.

Suffering is needed for enlightenment.
It will open your heart.
It will open your eyes.
It will set you free.

Let your suffering bring hope.
Let your suffering give wisdom.
Let your suffering follow My plan
  and end in peace and restful joy.

Let not your mind be tormented with concern.
Just allow your pain to be used.

Be peaceful in your pain,
  as it leads you to My land.
Come toward Me with your heart,
  as this direction belongs to you.
Deliver your pain to Me, as I will set you free.

Protection

PROTECTION

Protect yourself from discouragement,
    as it will lead you in a false direction.
Instead, be surrounded by hope
    and expectation for good.
Do not allow discouraged thinking to surround you.
If you are in its grasp,
    repel it and cover yourself
    with the armor of My protective grace.

Put on the strength of this protective grace.
Wear it as you face your enemy.

When you are injured,
    let My grace heal your wounds.
Allow this protection to become a part of you,
    and no fear will consume you.
No obstacle is too large for you to conquer.
No defeat will encompass you.

Be encouraged unto a new bravery with My protection,
    as no harm can consume you.
Let My protection lift your spirit
    and bring you face to face with My grace.

CONCERNS

My Spirit is for you.
My sacrifice lifts you.
What life exists without Me?
What future unfolds without Me?

Not a moment passes without My guidance.
Not an hour or a day would exist without My design.

Understand that you are My design
　and that your presence with those whom you know
best was initiated by me.

This should encourage you as each of your life's events
　brings you closer to the glory awaiting you.

Understand your experiences of life's time table
　and discover how much I am supporting you
　and guiding the unknown for you.

If you have all this, then what concerns should you bear
except false ones?

FLAME

Bring your brokenness to Me.
I will set you free.
Pour out the pain of your heart.
I will remove you from the test.
Welcome Me into your heart,
　for I am here for you to call.

What do you want of Me?
For what do you hunger?
Let your soul rest within Me.
Your peace is found in Me.
Let yourself come into My heart
　and become awakened by Its flame.

FOOTSTEPS

I am your strength,
    for I will protect you from what threatens you.
Let My protection cover you and give you courage
    and rest as you face your foes and enemies.

Let not your fear take a prominent place within your heart,
    as it does not accomplish My plan through you.
Have only courage then,
    as I am at your side.

I am your strength
    as you go forth with My work.
Why should you have fear
    if what I say is truth?
Take comfort in this question,
    as it is truth and My promise to you!

Let not your path be misdirected
    from the course I have set.
For your footsteps will not lead you
    in a false direction.

STAFF OF STRENGTH

Your love is pleasing.
Your praises are known in My kingdom.
Your suffering brings glory to all.

These actions do not harm you.
They bring comfort.
They manifest My presence.

Rejoice in these times,
    as My staff of strength will be upon you.
My Spirit will walk with you,
    and you will know My presence.

What doubt then should concern you?
What evil then will harm you?
My protection is all that is needed.

NO HARM WILL SURROUND YOU

What troubles surround you?
What difficulties block your path?
Do not worry or be concerned with these,
    as these situations are small to Me.

Place your trust in Me and trust My ways.
Not a minute will pass without My hand
    being present in these situations.

Not a day passes without My guidance
    being present over any difficulties.

Set your sight, then, on Me,
  and all obstacles will be removed.

All troubles will vanish.
Have faith in My protection.
For no harm will surround you.

Peace

PEACE

When you are together with those you love,
   I am joyful.
Use this time to praise Me and one another.
I want each of you to be peaceful
   with those to whom you are closest.
This peace is beyond what you think of
   when you relate its condition
   to your human understanding and relationships.
My peace is beyond your perceptions, anticipations,
   and understandings.

The peace I give to you is whole, not half.
The peace I give to you is light, not dark.
The peace I give to you is mine, not yours.

Take what I give to you
   and let this gift be for those closest to you.
You need not understand why you are blessed.
Take My peace with you and use it for others.

My peace will change and strengthen you.
My peace will bring you close to Me.
Ask for this.

Do not be afraid
   of the change that can be seen in you.
Do not be afraid
   to share this peace with those whom you are with.
I want to use you for this purpose.

Let Me be within you.
Let your words be My words.

My words will flow from you to those who need to hear.
Let Me use you. Let Me bless you.

CONTENTMENT IS YOURS

Your life's events yield questions
    that cannot be answered.
Believe that answers are present,
    but you cannot see them.

What matters is not your full awareness
    but only your trust and faith.
Focus then on your trust in goodness.
Release your doubts and questioning,
    as these are not helpful.
Set your fears aside
    and open your heart to My methods.

Trust that My goodness is present
    amongst human confusion.
Trust that My hand directs life's events.
With this belief, then,
    what concerns are necessary?
With this faith, then,
    only a happy heart should remain.

Life's burdens should not own you.
Let these burdens
    be released unto encouragement.
Let My words
    lift your heart unto joy and peace.
Let these rewards
    fill your heart with contentment.

LIFE TO DEATH

The human condition that I have created
  is for all to understand
  the new life that awaits them.
Do not think that it is the same experience
  as your humanity.
It is not.

Do not anticipate what this new life consists of;
  you are unable to understand it.
Know only that it is peace-filled
  and more than you now encounter and have.
It is like no other.

You will enjoy this time with Me
  when it is delivered to you.
I will care for you
  when this experience is given to you.
Look forward to this event
  and do not fear the unknown.
I give you peace-filled moments in your human life
  so you may begin to know
  what spiritual treasures await you.

NEW LIFE

Let new life surround you
  as you look for answers.
Let new life give you freedom
  as you trust in My ways.

No time escapes you
  when your purpose is focused upon Me.
No event escapes you
  when you place your thoughts toward Me.
No message is unknown to you
  as you submit yourself unto Me.

Take joy from your pain for Me,
  as its reward awaits you.
Be content with the peacefulness I give unto you,
  as this blessing is bestowed.

SPIRITUAL GIFTS AND GIVING

This time you have is a gift from Me.
Use it with great care,
  as it will end as I decide.
Use this gift to provide for others.
Help them enjoy their gifts,
  as I do for you.

May you seek your gifts from Me.
May you bring a wealth of happiness
  to those around you.
What greater giving can be found than this?

Bring peace to those with whom you come in contact.
Give joy and peace to them.
Bring life to those who suffer pain.
Help them pass over this time of suffering.

Be gentle with those who are angry with their situations.
Bring wisdom to them as they cross your path.
Let compassion show forth from your eyes
    and cross over into their pain.
Your strength will heal their pain.

I bring them to you for healing.
Let My strength pass over into them.
These people need My strength.
Let Me use you for this purpose.

THE FRUIT OF PEACE

You look for pleasure
    and find brief satisfaction.
Your search continues,
    and you fail.

Come to Me for your pleasure
    and have My peace.
It awaits you.

My peace will fill you with many fruits
    and lift your burdens.
It will cover and protect you.

My peace will ease your pain
    and strengthen you.

Do not fear its favor,
   as its blessings will not harm you.

It will heal your pain
   and ease your anguish.
It will set you free.
It will bring new wisdom and understanding.

This gift of My peace is yours
   when you come to Me.
Take its fruits
   and let it help you.

Surrender

A SERVANT'S SUBMISSION

Become My servant,
  and I will lead you.
Be present to My promptings,
  and I will show you.
Be aware of My voice in others
  and recognize its suggestions.
Listen to Me when I speak.
Hear Me when I lead you.

What fear merits your attention when I guide you?
What concern should you hold of My direction?

Submit to Me,
  and I will show you.
Turn to Me,
  and your fear will diminish.
Come to Me
  and enjoy My favor.
Look to Me
  and find your answers.

I wait for your submission.
I am anxious for your surrender.
Do this
  and bring joy to My purpose for you.
Enjoy its result
  and be blessed by its fruits.

What delays warrant your attention?
What other goal or vision exists than My favor?

Turn to Me
   and accept your gifts that await you.
Submit your purpose to Me
   and be filled with peace.

Let My peace fill you, change you, lift you,
   and open your heart to Me.
Let My peace heal you of your wounds
   and comfort you each day.
Let My peace open the eyes of your blindness
   and bring knowledge into your darkness.
Accept My purpose for you
   and trust that I will enlighten you.
Become My servant,
   and you will know Me.

A VISION

What do you see
   when your visions are focused upon Me?
What do you see
   when you become My servant?
What do you have
   without a vision of Me?
What have you gained
   without Me as your Master?

Invite Me into your visions
   and see Me more clearly.
Invite Me into your life
   and let Me become your God.

I AM the end of your search.
I AM the light that does not darken with time.
I AM your treasure!
Walk with Me;
   talk with Me;
   listen to Me;
   and you will know Me.

Let Me convince you that I AM all that is.
I AM your God that was, is, and will be with you.

Invite Me to be with you,
   and your vision will reach into My nature.
Invite Me to be with you,
   and you will know Me.

LETTING GO

Life cannot be controlled by you.
You cannot guide its path.
Let go of its wheel and turn its path toward Me.
Its course will be set,
   and its sails will not be broken.
I will turn its wheels as needed,
   when your course is set toward My path.

With this direction set,
   then what doubt should you have?
With this course,
   then what worry should you possess?
Let not your time be wasted with other directions.
Letting go will lead you into the waters of My land.

PATIENCE

The hours of each day test your patience
   with life's conflicts.
Bring hope and peace to these tests.

Let your peacefulness bring a glow unto any conflict.
Your character is tested so you may conquer the test.

Let these times lift your hopes
   and enlighten your dreams.
Enjoy the conflict,
   as it is created for your growth.
Do not give in to its shadow of darkness.
Bring your being into My light.

Let this light lift your spirit
   and fill you with new
   dreams, hopes, and peacefulness.
Own the benefits of these gifts,
   as you need not concern yourself
   with its reason or justification.

Take what I give to you as My gift.
Let the fruits of My gifts
   be placed within you.
Allow the light of these fruits
   to penetrate your spirit.

SEARCHING

Confusion will reside
  whenever you search for sources of acceptance
  other than Me.
Keep your focus upon Me,
  and all other things will be taken care of.

Direction is given
  to those who seek this from Me.
You leave Me and then return again.
My direction will also leave and return.

I want you to come to Me more often.
I know this is difficult,
  and you cannot always achieve this.
Strive for increasing the frequency
  of this closeness to Me.
Your confusion will pass
  as you accept Me more often.

What gain does a man have
  who has everything
  but does not know Me?
What direction will he take?

He will lose himself within his own selfish desires.
He will become confused, desperate,
  and continue a search for more of the same.
This man is lost,
  and his search will lead him to despair.

Let this man reach out for Me,
  and he will find his way.
He will know Me.

Let this man search for Me,
   and he will find Me.
Let this man find Me
   and what he is will be changed.

What gain does a man have
   who does not reach out for Me.
I am what he is missing.

Let him come to Me with his mind and heart.
I will give him all that he needs.
His search will end,
   and he will know Me.

THE TIME OF YOUR LIFE

Your time is spent for life's events.
Examine this time and trace its source.
Do you know its source?
Is it from Me?

Let Me have your time.
Let Me enter into your heart's direction.
Allow Me to conquer your path.
Surrender yourself and allow Me to direct your way.

I await your surrender each day.
Let Me be within you each day.

Do you waste time?
Do you not recognize Me each day?
Change your path and direct it toward Me.
Give yourself to Me.

If you surrender,
    then you have conquered.
If you give up your unjust desires,
    then you have joined me.
Let yourself be free.
Let yourself live in My purpose,
    as I await your gift of time.

Comfort

COMFORT

My life was for you.
My death set you free.
Take comfort in this
  as you are My child.
Live as My children
  and know that you are of My Father's hand.
Be encouraged by this promise
  and enjoy its favor.
Yield to its fruits
  and let them touch you.
Welcome My Father's favor
  and let these fruits cover you.

You search and find despair.
You question and discover nothing.
Speak with Me
  and find the comfort you search for.
Question Me
  and discover the plan for you,
  for within it lies your answers.

Your eyes can be opened.
Your heart can be softened.
Your despair can be changed.
Let your search end with Me.
Let your difficulties find their end in Me.
End your despair.
Find what you seek in Me.

Let your difficulties diminish
  as you take comfort in My promises.
My comfort awaits your surrender.

Let its fruits enter you, encourage you,
  and bring you peace.

ACCEPTANCE

Life is only what happens during your time on Earth.
Much more awaits those who yield to its path.
If you are stricken,
  do not despair.
Let My grace comfort your condition.
Do not fear an evil outcome,
  as I am always with you.
Life's events mean little
  for those who seek everlasting time with Me.

Accept your status,
  as it is meant for you.
Let not fear or mistrust surround you.
I am always at your side
  as you call upon My name.

CARING

My peace will cover your heart.
My grace will lift your spirit.
Take joy from this protection.
Be comforted by its promises,
  as I fulfill My Words.

Let nothing disrupt your trust.
Let no fear or distraction mislead you.

I see your suffering.
I know of your pain.
I listen to your questions.
I care for you.

Oh child of mine,
    I am with you always.
I am never beyond your reach.
Nothing can distract My care for you.

DELIVERANCE

In times of difficulty,
    I am with you.
See My hands guiding and helping.
Do not be afraid of this deliverance,
    as it will lead you to the end chosen for you.

Set yourself free from hesitation and doubt,
    as these are not from Me;
    they will only distract you.
Lift your eyes and heart to Me,
    as My work is fulfilled in you.

My work will guide and instruct you
    as you surrender to My plan.
Take comfort then in the outcome,
    as it pleases Me.
Do not concern yourself with the path of My plan,
    as its end will bring you peace and contentment.

EXPERIENCE MY COMFORT

Each experience you encounter
  can bring new awareness.
Let this awareness encourage your view of life's failings.

Look for good in place of disappointment.
See the hope that can feed others.
Take the benefits for new enlightenment.
Let encouragement fill you with goodness.
Let hope lift you unto a new direction.
Let My direction place you into My hands
  and bring you comfort.

Notes:

Notes:

Notes:

Notes:

29112540R00075